HOCKEY'S
BEST SHOTS

THE GREATEST NHL® PHOTOGRAPHY OF THE CENTURY

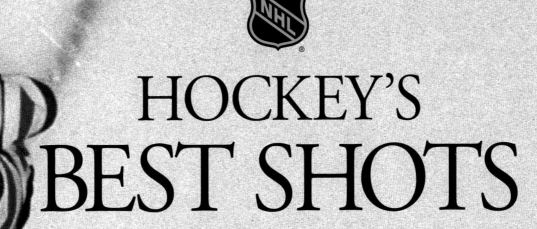

HOCKEY'S
BEST SHOTS

THE GREATEST NHL® PHOTOGRAPHY OF THE CENTURY

FOREWORD BY GORDIE AND COLLEEN HOWE, MR. & MRS. HOCKEY®

A BALLIETT & FITZGERALD BOOK

DK PUBLISHING
www.dk.com

HOCKEY'S BEST SHOTS

 A DK PUBLISHING BOOK

First American Edition, 2001

00 01 02 03 04 05 10 9 8 7 6 5 4 3 2 1

DK Publishing, Inc.
95 Madison Avenue,
New York, NY 10016
Fax: 800-600-9098.

A catalog record for this book is available from the Library of Congress

Color reproduction by ColourScan, Singapore
Printed and bound in Spain by Artes Gráficas Toledo S.A.U.
D.L. TO: 716 - 2001

 ## NATIONAL HOCKEY LEAGUE®

A Balliett & Fitzgerald Book

Editor: Chris Allard
Designers: Mark Kehoe, Michael Walters
Production Managers: Maria Fernandez, Simon M. Sullivan,
Michael Walters
Photo Research: Mary Fran Loftus, Omni-Photo
Communications, Inc.

DK Publishing, Inc.:
Publisher: Sean Moore
Editorial Director: Chuck Wills
Art Director: Tina Vaughan

We would like to thank Denise Gomez, Manager of Printed
Products—NHL; Frank Brown, V.P. of Media Relations—
NHL; Arthur Pincus, Editorial Consultant to the NHL;
and NHL Images for their creative input and assistance in
making this project possible.

PRE-GAME SPLITS

PAGE 1

TORONTO MAPLE LEAFS GOALIE CURTIS
JOSEPH, KNOWN FOR HIS ACROBATICS,
LIMBERS UP BEFORE A CONTEST
AGAINST BUFFALO AND THE EQUALLY
NIMBLE DOMINIK HASEK.

CRAIG MELVIN/NHL IMAGES 2000

EDMONTON ASSISTANCE

PREVIOUS PAGES

EDMONTON OILERS DEFENSEMEN
KEVIN LOWE AND CRAIG MUNI COME TO
GOALIE GRANT FUHR'S ASSISTANCE.

DAVID E. KLUTHO/ICON SPORTS MEDIA
1987

WELCOME BACK

NEXT PAGE

MARIO LEMIEUX OF THE PITTSBURGH
PENGUINS ACKNOWLEDGES HIS FANS
ON THE NIGHT OF HIS RETURN FROM A
THREE-YEAR RETIREMENT—A NIGHT
WORTH ONE GOAL AND TWO ASSISTS
FOR LEMIEUX IN A 5-0 VICTORY OVER
TORONTO.

M. DAVID LEEDS/ALLSPORT 2000

FOREWORD

BY GORDIE AND COLLEEN HOWE, MR. & MRS. HOCKEY®

HOCKEY HAS NEVER BEEN JUST ABOUT GOALS, just as baseball has never been just about home runs and strikeout pitches; and as we scanned the spellbinding collection of photos in this splendid book, we could see hockey's history and tradition unfold. The sights, smells, and sounds of hockey are as comforting to a player as anything else he knows. To a player, the arena is more like a cathedral than a workplace. He loves to be there paying homage to a sport that means the world to him. The wonder of this book is that it allows the fan to pull back the curtain and to share in hockey's intimate details. That's why we love the page 12 picture of the equipment man dumping pucks onto the ice for practice or Stan Mikita shaving his banana curve stick on page 37. Fans probably don't realize that an NHL player treats his stick with the same reverence that a carpenter has for his tools.

These pictures tell you as much about hockey as you could learn if we spent hour after hour telling you stories about the game. You can almost hear the ice being churned into a snowy spray with the terrific shot of Pierre Turgeon and Jiri Slegr on pages 26-27. You can sense the speed of the game simply by seeing Guy Lafleur's hair flow behind him as he jets up ice on page 55 or the blurred shot of Derek Plante as he engages warp speed on page 56.

If you want to appreciate how difficult it is to score a goal during a mad scramble in front of the net, simply look at "All Sticks Converging" on page 30. If you want to know how tough this game can be, turn to page 75 and see the price Dave Andreychuk paid to be in scoring position. To understand the richness of hockey's tradition, look at the 1951 photo of Ted Kennedy meeting then-Princess Elizabeth at Maple Leaf Gardens on page 40.

Hockey's humanity also comes through with the timeless images of Toe Blake and Scotty Bowman behind the bench, or our dear friend, Wayne Gretzky, signing autographs when he was a baby-faced Edmonton Oilers' star, or Mario Lemieux smiling at his friend and teammate Ron Francis on page 16.

The classic image of Boston Bruins center Phil Esposito skating toward his brother Tony in the Chicago net on pages 34-35 has a special place in our hearts because we know firsthand what it means to have the sport intertwined with

BETWEEN THE WHA AND THE NHL, GORDIE HOWE AND SONS MARK (L) AND MARTY (R) PLAYED SEVEN SEASONS AND TWO CHAMPIONSHIPS TOGETHER —PHOTO COURTESY OF NORMAN JAMES

family relationships. The highlight of our long tenure in hockey came during the 1973-74 season when Gordie was able to skate for the Houston Aeros on a line with our sons Mark and Marty.

Hockey can be both a cruel game and a beautiful game all within a span of several seconds. One moment a player can be executing a perfectly choreographed passing play when skating 20 mph and the next minute he can be unleashing a bodycheck to prevent a counter-attack. But when we turn the pages and look at all of these dramatic photos, it's like turning the pages of a family album to us. The athletes depicted in these photos are all our friends—truly like members of our family: Frank Mahovlich, Alex Delvecchio, Bobby Orr, Glenn Hall, Lorne "Gump" Worsley, Henri Richard, Johnny Bower. When we leaf through these photos, what comes to mind is how fiercely we competed against each and yet how much we respected each other.

What this book really does is give fans a chance to get inside our fraternity house for just a short period. To appreciate the jubilation and joy that can come from living in this world, look at page 13 as the Toronto Maple Leafs celebrate winning the

GORDIE HOWE IS STILL THE ALL-TIME REGULAR SEASON SCORING CHAMP FOR THE NHL AND WHA COMBINED. GRAPHIC ARTISTS/HOCKEY HALL OF FAME 1968

Stanley Cup in 1947. The Howe family has known that overflowing level of emotion many times over, even when we weren't winning championships. This sport is special, and it has special people. We have loved our six decades of participation in this grand game.

One of our favorite photos in the book is the page 47 shot of Worsley shaking hands with Bower after a hotly contested playoff series. Minutes before, those guys were heated adversaries. They probably would have done anything to beat each other. But now that the series was over, they greeted each other warmly. It was just two warriors acknowledging the admiration they had for one another.

That's the hockey world that the Howe family knows. We hope that *Hockey's Best Shots* gives you a better understanding of it. Enjoy it! ∎

Gordie Howe®, Mr. Hockey®, is widely recognized as the greatest all-around hockey player in history. His pro career spanned an unbelievable 32 seasons and covered 6 decades. When he retired from the sport, he held more records than any athlete in history, having established all-time marks for goals, assists, points, games played, and game-winning goals. Often considered the most durable athlete in history, he had his best seasons at the ages of 41 and 48. Mr. Hockey® has appeared in 29 All-Star games and was in the top 5 (NHL) in scoring for an unbelievable 20 consecutive years.

His wife, Colleen Howe, Mrs. Hockey™, is the most influential woman in the history of hockey. Together, Gordie and Colleen Howe, Mr. & Mrs. Hockey®, are recognized around the world as the game's greatest couple. Colleen is the first female member of the U.S. Hockey Hall-Of-Fame. Since 1953, she has spearheaded her family's operations, which include Power Play International, Inc., Power Play Publications, Inc., and the Howe Foundation. She serves as president of all family organizations.

INTRODUCTION

BY GARY B. BETTMAN, COMMISSIONER, NATIONAL HOCKEY LEAGUE

HOCKEY'S BEST SHOTS: *The Greatest NHL Photography of the Century* is a remarkable book filled with remarkable photographs of a remarkable sport. This collection, which includes photos that date back more than half a century, captures the spirit and competitiveness of our great athletes and the game they play. This book also is a tribute to the photographers whose craftsmanship will captivate newcomers and long-time fans alike.

In addition to the scores of talented photographers whose works are displayed on these pages, this marvelous array of hockey images also owes its existence to the dedicated group of archivists and historians who have tended, catalogued, and preserved these treasures through the years. Though their work often goes unsung, it cannot be applauded too strongly.

From its inception in 1943, the Hockey Hall of Fame has compiled an outstanding photo archive, beginning with glass-plate images, progressing into the speed film era, and advancing into today's age of digital photography.

The photographic heritage of our game has been enhanced particularly by the private collections of the legendary Turofsky brothers, Lou and Nat, and Harold Barkley in Toronto, David Bier and Denis Brodeur in Montreal, and Bruce Bennett in New York. Their works contribute greatly to this living legacy. Hockey is forever indebted to their talents and the many other artists who with such skill, season after season, have preserved even the most intimate details of our games.

In paging through *Hockey's Best Shots: The Greatest NHL Photography of the Century*, I was struck not only by the great images but also by the fact that there are so many photographs of the great NHL stars through the years.

The editors have captured the essence, the very soul, of hockey. There are great celebrations and moments of profound despair, thoughtful "mood" shots that visit the personality of the game, officials in action, and great coaches at work. There is something for everyone.

For a hockey fan, *Hockey's Best Shots: The Greatest NHL Photography of the Century*, is a timeless treasure—something to be visited and re-visited, something to be enjoyed and then enjoyed again…just like the game itself. ■

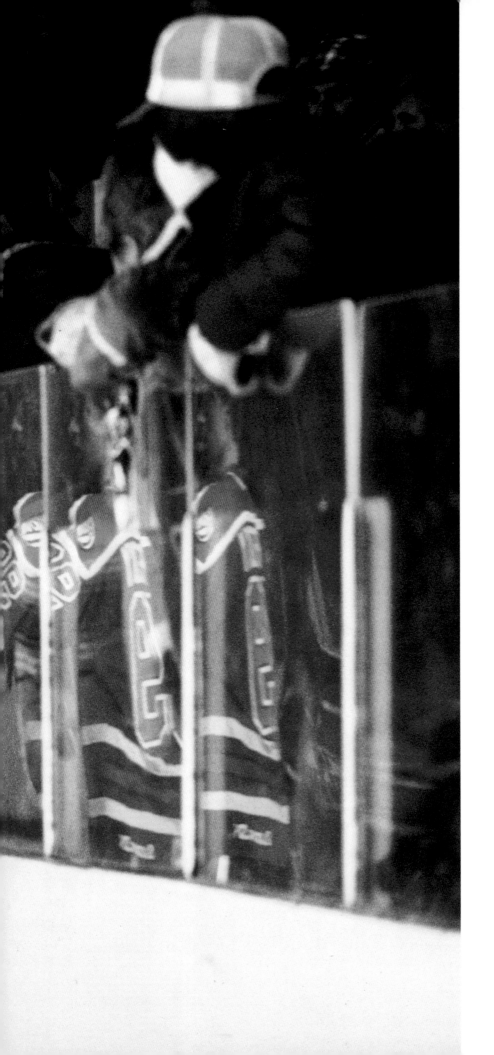

FAN TIME

WAYNE GRETZKY, SEEN HERE EARLY IN HIS
CAREER, TAKES A FEW MOMENTS DURING
A PRE-GAME WORKOUT TO SIGN
AUTOGRAPHS FOR FANS, A RITUAL HE
WILL HONOR THROUGHOUT HIS CAREER.
LONDON LIFE—PORTNOY/
HOCKEY HALL OF FAME EARLY 1980S

FEEDING TIME
Practice means a bucket of pucks.
Craig Melvin/NHL Images

THE WINNING TEAM
As the final buzzer officially declares
them Stanley Cup champions over
the Montreal Canadiens, the Toronto
Maple Leafs storm the ice.
Imperial Oil—Turofsky/Hockey Hall of Fame 1947

PARDON ME

Nik Antropov of the Toronto Maple Leafs skips and stumbles around a New York Ranger in an effort to maintain control of the puck.

Dave Sandford/NHL images 2000

MARIO & CO.

FAMOUSLY COOL, ESPECIALLY AS THEY LED
PITTSBURGH TO STANLEY CUP WINS IN
1991 AND 1992, PENGUINS MARIO LEMIEUX
AND RON FRANCIS ALLOW THEMSELVES
SOME LEVITY DURING A PRE-GAME WARM-UP.
STEVE BABINEAU/SPORTS ACTION MID-'90S

CAVALCADE

WITH DETROIT RED WING SERGEI FEDOROV (91)
AWAITING A PASS THAT COULD SEND HIM IN
ON THE TORONTO NET, THE MAPLE LEAFS MOUNT
A MASS RUSH BACK, LED BY DIMITRY
YUSHKEVICH (36) AND DANNY MARKOV (55).
MATTHEW MANOR/HOCKEY HALL OF FAME 2000

FREEZE FRAME

Mounted behind the net, the photographer's
flash zaps Toronto Maple Leaf Paul
Henderson and Montreal defenseman
Terry Harper, and goalie Lorne Worsley.
Graphic Artists/Hockey Hall of Fame 1969

NO DOUBT ABOUT IT

Florida Panther Tom Fitzgerald holds nothing
back after putting the puck past Philadelphia
Flyer netminder Tommy Soderstrom.
Bruce Bennett Studios 1993-94

TRUE SPIRIT

THE BRIGHT, OVERHEAD ARENA LIGHTS MAKE
THE DETROIT RED WINGS BENCH
LOOK LIKE AN ARMY OF VERITABLE WARRIORS
WHEN CAST ONTO THE POWDERY ICE SURFACE.
CRAIG MELVIN/NHL IMAGES 1998

THE POSE
NOTED THROUGHOUT THE HOCKEY WORLD FOR
HIS PRETZEL MASK AND HIS RESTING POSE,
MONTREAL CANADIEN KEN DRYDEN WILL GO ON TO
WIN SIX STANLEY CUPS IN ONLY EIGHT SEASONS AND
FINISH HIS CAREER AS THE GOALIE WITH THE HIGHEST
WINNING PERCENTAGE.
M. DiGiacomo/Bruce Bennett Studios 1972

GONE

SIX FEET, FOUR INCHES TALL AND ARMED WITH A
DANGEROUS REACH, MARIO LEMIEUX HAS THE
UNCANNY ABILITY TO FREE HIMSELF FROM MOST PLAYERS.
STEVE BABINEAU/SPORTS ACTION MID-1990S

BALLETIC BOWER

JOHNNY "THE CHINA WALL" BOWER, WHO SPENT EIGHT
YEARS IN THE MINORS BEFORE MAKING IT TO
THE NHL, DEMONSTRATES THE SKILLS THAT PUT
HIM INTO THE HALL OF FAME.
IMPERIAL OIL—TUROFSKY/HOCKEY HALL OF FAME EARLY 1960S

TOP SHELF

Montreal Canadien Henri "The Pocket Rocket"
Richard picks his spot over the left shoulder of
Toronto Maple Leaf netminder Johnny Bower.
Imperial Oil—Turofsky/Hockey Hall of Fame early 1960s

CAT AND MOUSE

St. Louis Blue Pierre Turgeon
and Pittsburgh Penguin Jiri
Slegr both kick up showers of
snow as they come to full stops
and switch directions.
Elsa Hasch/AllSport 2000

THE MAN IN CHARGE

Scotty Bowman, the winningest coach in NHL history—with stints in St. Louis, Montreal, Buffalo, Pittsburgh, and Detroit—mulls over his next move in the dying moments of a game.
Bruce Bennett/Bruce Bennett Studios mid-1990s

MASKED MAGICIAN

One month after first donning a mask in a game, Montreal Canadien Jacques Plante snares a shot and holds off Bob Pulford of the Toronto Maple Leafs.
Imperial Oil—Turofsky/Hockey Hall of Fame 1959

ALL STICKS CONVERGING

Defenseman Brian Leetch of the New York
Rangers seems hopelessly trapped
in a tangle of Washington Capitals sticks.
J. Giamundo/Bruce Bennett Studios 2000

THE SHOT THAT
WON THE 1970 CUP

AFTER SCORING ON ST.LOUIS BLUES GOALIE
GLENN HALL TO GIVE THE BOSTON BRUINS
THE STANLEY CUP IN OVERTIME, BOBBY ORR DIVES
FOR JOY—UNINTENTIONALLY, IT TURNS OUT, BECAUSE
DEFENSEMAN NOEL PICARD, IN THE BACKGROUND, HAS
JUST TRIPPED HIM.
FRED KENNAN/HOCKEY HALL OF FAME 1970

BRO VS BRO
Boston Bruin Phil Esposito is left alone in the slot. Guarding against him in the net? His brother Tony of the Chicago Blackhawks.
Bruce Bennett Studios 1971

O'CALLAHAN
CANADIEN
7000
MURRAY 6
MURRAY 6
BALANCED
FRASER
DONNELLY
DONNELLY
FEATH
S.O.P.
STAPELTON
WATSON
KOHO

CHICAGO RACK

RULE 19: STICKS SHALL NOT EXCEED 63"
FROM TIP TO HEEL OR 12.5"
FROM HEEL TO THE END OF THE BLADE.
DAVID E. KLUTHO/ICON SMI 1986

THE MIKITA BANANA

WITH CONTROL AND SHOT SPEED INFLUENCED
BY THE CURVE OF A STICK BLADE,
CHICAGO BLACKHAWK STAN MIKITA DOES
SOME PRE-GAME CUSTOMIZING. HE WILL FINISH
THE 1966-67 SEASON ATOP THE SCORING LIST
AND WIN MVP HONORS.
GRAPHIC ARTISTS/HOCKEY HALL OF FAME 1966-67

ICED

FAMOUS FOR HIS CREATIVITY AND UNORTHODOX
STYLE OF PLAY, DOMINIK "THE DOMINATOR"
HASEK STILL LOSES THE OCCASIONAL
ONE, AS ON THIS PLAY WHEN AN OPPONENT'S
SHOT FINDS THE BACK OF THE NET.
IHA/ICON SMI 1998-99

ROYALTY IN THE HOUSE

TED KENNEDY, CAPTAIN OF THE TORONTO
MAPLE LEAFS, EXTENDS A PRE-GAME WELCOME
TO A VISITING PRINCESS ELIZABETH, WHO IS
ACCOMPANIED BY PRINCE PHILIP (TOP LEFT).
IMPERIAL OIL—TUROFSKY/HOCKEY HALL OF FAME 1951

GLOW IN THE DARK

THE FLASH FROM BEHIND THE NET LIGHTS UP THE
PUCK ABOVE TORONTO GOALIE JOHNNY BOWER, AS
TEAMMATE JOHNNY WILSON AND BOSTON BRUIN
JOHNNY BUCYK STAND TRANSFIXED IN THE SLOT.
IMPERIAL OIL—TUROFSKY/HOCKEY HALL OF FAME 1959

OUT OF SYNC

THE NEW YORK AMERICANS SQUAD,
WEARING THE WHITE JERSEYS, SEEMS
DISORIENTED AS THE DETROIT RED WINGS KEEP
THE PRESSURE ON DEEP IN THE ZONE.
HOCKEY HALL OF FAME 1940

LOOSE PUCK

WITH NEW YORK RANGERS DEFENSEMAN DUKE
DUKOWSKI CHECKING HIM, MONTREAL
CANADIEN HOWIE MORENZ—SEEN HERE IN A
RARE ACTION PHOTOGRAPH—TRIES TO
PUT THE PUCK PAST GOALIE ANDY AITKENHEAD.
HOCKEY HALL OF FAME 1934

REACH VS. REACH

New York Ranger goalie Ed Giacomin, noted
for his acrobatics, coolly drops to his
knees to poke-check Montreal Canadien Henri
Richard, who is trailed by Jean Ratelle.
Frank Prazak/Hockey Hall of Fame circa 1965

MAESTRO

HAVING SUFFERED A FOUR-SEASON DROUGHT AFTER
WINNING FIVE CHAMPIONSHIPS IN HIS FIRST
FIVE YEARS AS COACH OF THE MONTREAL
CANADIENS, TOE BLAKE FINDS HIMSELF ON THE
PLAYOFF-WINNING ROAD ONCE MORE, JUST A COUPLE
OF SERIES FROM ANOTHER STANLEY CUP.
BRUCE BENNETT STUDIOS 1965

THE SPORTING THING

RIVALS THROUGH MUCH OF THEIR CAREERS,
GOALTENDERS LORNE "GUMP" WORSLEY
OF THE NEW YORK RANGERS AND JOHNNY BOWER
OF THE TORONTO MAPLE LEAFS SHAKE
HANDS AT THE END OF A PLAYOFF SERIES.
IMPERIAL OIL—TUROFSKY/HOCKEY HALL OF FAME 1962

MAN WITH A RECORD
WAYNE GRETZKY FACES EVEN MORE LENSES THAN
USUAL AFTER BECOMING THE NHL'S ALL-TIME
LEADING SCORER WITH HIS 802ND CAREER GOAL,
TOPPING THE PREVIOUS MARK SET BY
GORDIE HOWE.
AL BELLO/ALLSPORT 1994

WILL IT?
ST. LOUIS BLUE FLOYD THOMSON, UPENDED BY
THE ENEMY GOALIE, CAN ONLY WATCH
AS THE PUCK SKIRTS THROUGH THE CREASE.
LONDON LIFE—PORTNOY/HOCKEY HALL OF FAME CIRCA 1974

DUCK
WITH A SKIP AND A JUMP, RON MURPHY
OF THE NEW YORK RANGERS
AVOIDS A COLLISION WITH HIS OWN
GOALIE, LORNE WORSLEY.
HERB SCHARFMAN/©BETTMANN/CORBIS 1955

GUT SAVE

His angles sealed, goalie Ron Hextall of the Philadelphia Flyers takes a Steve Yzerman shot in the crest of his jersey during the Stanley Cup finals against the Detroit Red Wings.

Bruce Bennett Studios 1997

ROAD TO THE CUP
The training-camp conditioning of
the 1931-32 Toronto Maple Leafs ultimately
led to a Stanley Cup championship.
Imperial Oil—Turofsky/Hockey Hall of Fame 1931

FLOWER POWER
In typically lithe fashion, Montreal
Canadien Guy Lafleur turns on the jets.
Bruce Bennett Studios 1982

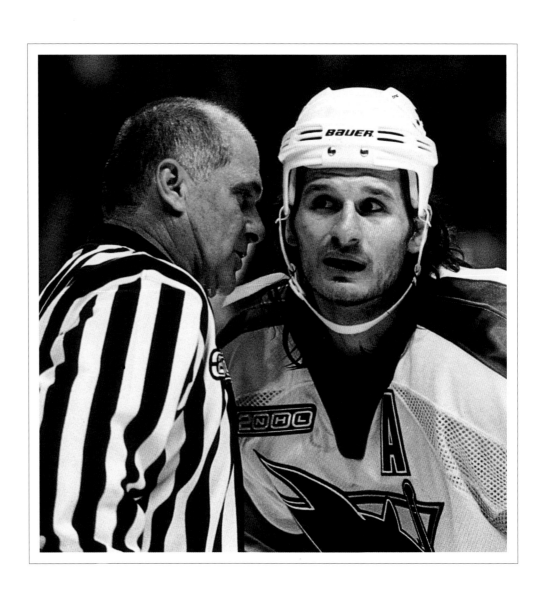

AT DIZZYING SPEED
It's neck-and-neck between Buffalo Sabre Derek Plante and a Philadelphia Flyer during first-round playoff action.
Aubrey Washington/Allsport 1998

THE EXPLANATION
An attentive Mike Ricci of the San Jose Sharks receives clarification of a call from linesman Ray Scapinello.
Donald Miralle/Allsport 2000

SEEDS OF GREATNESS

BOSTON BRUINS COACH HARRY SINDEN STANDS
BEHIND HIS CHARGES, AMONG THEM
A YOUNG PHIL ESPOSITO (AT CENTER) WHO
IN THE LATE 1960S IS EMERGING AS
THE TOP OFFENSIVE FORCE IN THE NHL.
FRANK PRAZAK/HOCKEY HALL OF FAME 1967-68

THE SAVE'S THE THING

WITH A PAIR OF TORONTO OPPONENTS ROAMING
BY, RED WINGS GOALIE TERRY SAWCHUK
RISKS ALL, INCLUDING INJURY TO HIS
FACE, TO KEEP THE PUCK OUT OF HIS NET.
IMPERIAL OIL—TUROFSKY/HOCKEY HALL OF FAME 1960

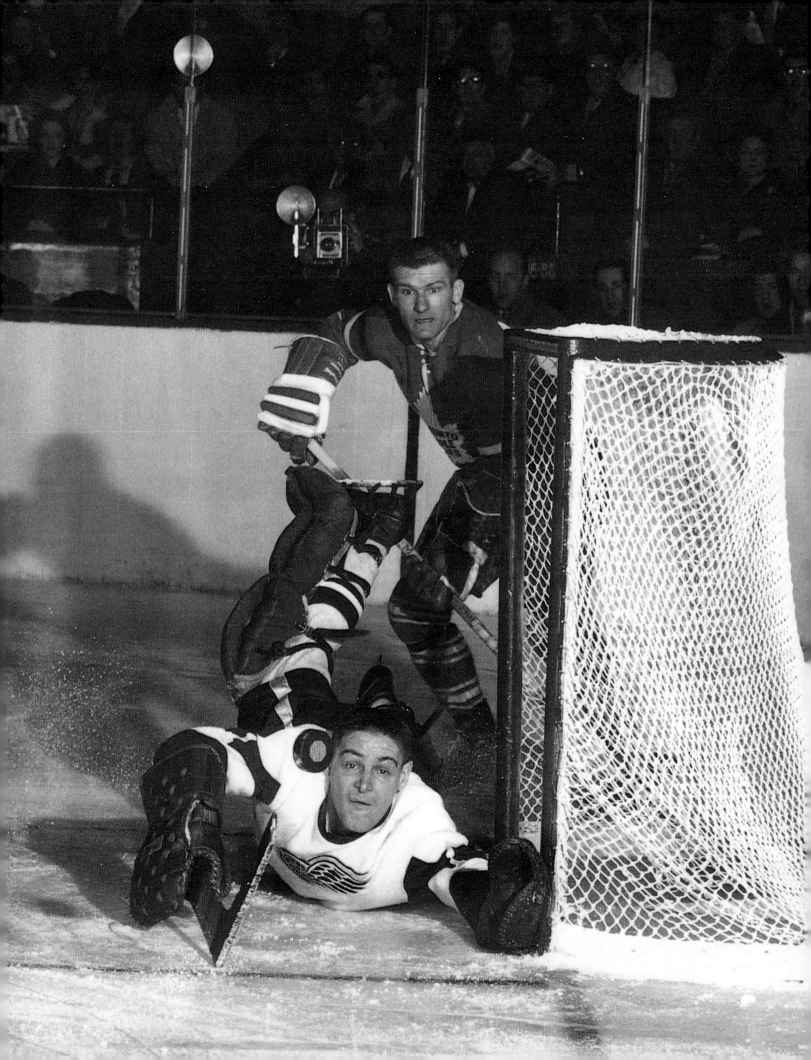

PUCK DOWN BELOW
CORY CROSS OF THE TAMPA BAY LIGHTNING AND
CHRIS CHELIOS OF THE CHICAGO
BLACKHAWKS GO ONE-ON-ONE IN THE CORNER.
STEVE BABINEAU/SPORTS ACTION 1997-98

SQUEEZE PLAY
IT'S UP-CLOSE AND PERSONAL FOR SOME
TORONTO FANS AS, INCHES AWAY, DETROIT RED
WING BOB GOLDHAM SQUEEZES MAPLE LEAFS
CAPTAIN JIM MORRISON AGAINST THE BOARDS.
IMPERIAL OIL—TUROFSKY/
HOCKEY HALL OF FAME 1955

FIXTURES
ONE-TIME OPPONENTS IN US COLLEGE
HOCKEY, DEFENSEMAN KEITH MAGNUSON
AND GOALIE TONY ESPOSITO STRIKE A POSE
THAT WILL REMAIN FAMILIAR TO CHICAGO
BLACKHAWKS FANS FOR MORE
THAN A DECADE, BEGINNING IN 1969.
LONDON LIFE—PORTNOY/HOCKEY HALL OF FAME 1974

THE SHOT THAT
WON THE 1951 CUP
BILL BARILKO SAILS THROUGH THE AIR, HIS SHOT
HAVING JUST ENTERED THE NET OVER
THE SHOULDER OF GOALIE GERRY MCNEIL,
INSTANTLY GIVING THE TORONTO
MAPLE LEAFS THE CHAMPIONSHIP IN OVERTIME
OVER THE MONTREAL CANADIENS.
IMPERIAL OIL—TUROFSKY/HOCKEY HALL OF FAME 1951

COOL DOWN
MONTREAL CANADIEN NETMINDER JEFF
HACKETT REFUELS DURING A BREAK IN THE ACTION.
CRAIG MELVIN/NHL IMAGES 2000

POISED

New York Rangers goalie Gilles Villemure
stands in position in his crease as the puck
drops in the face-off circle.
Bruce Bennett Studios early 1970s

UPENDED

Despite having his feet knocked out
from under him, Toronto Maple Leaf
Frank Mahovlich still manages a shot on
Detroit Red Wings goalie Terry Sawchuk.
Imperial Oil—Turofsky/
Hockey Hall of Fame 1960-61

OLD PALS

Ex-teammates Glenn Healy of Toronto
and Steve Sullivan of Chicago
catch up on the news since Sullivan's trade
to the Blackhawks at the start of
1999-2000 season, five months earlier.
Dave Sandford/NHL Images 2000

HARD RIGHT

PIT MARTIN OF THE BOSTON BRUINS LEANS
INTO HIS TURN BEFORE TRYING
TO CUT AROUND MAPLE LEAFS DEFENSEMAN
TIM HORTON DEEP IN THE TORONTO ZONE.
FRANK PRAZAK/HOCKEY HALL OF FAME 1966-67

TRAFFIC REPORT
As confusion seems to rule among the
players around his crease,
New York Ranger goalie Jason Muzzatti
tries to sneak a poke at the puck.
Bruce Bennett Studios 1997

TOP MAN
Detroit Red Wing Gordie Howe contains his
emotions despite having just become the top
goal scorer of all time with his 545th
career goal, one more than Maurice Richard.
Next to him is team captain Alex Delvecchio.
©Bettmann/Corbis 1963

GOOOAAAALLLLLL!!!!

MONTREAL CANADIEN YVAN COURNOYER NETS
ONE AGAINST TORONTO NETMINDER JOHNNY
BOWER AS CANADIENS CAPTAIN JEAN BELIVEAU
AND MAPLE LEAFS ALLEN STANLEY (26)
AND KENT DOUGLAS (19) EXAMINE THE DAMAGE.
GRAPHIC ARTISTS/HOCKEY HALL OF FAME MID-1960S

RISKY VENTURE

TREADING A LITTLE TOO CLOSE TO THE ENEMY
GOAL CREASE, TORONTO MAPLE LEAF
DAVE ANDREYCHUK CROSSES PATHS
WITH RUGGED DEFENSEMAN ROB BLAKE
OF THE LOS ANGELES KINGS.
DOUG MACLELLAN/HOCKEY HALL OF FAME 1993

FINALLY, VICTORY
JOE SAKIC ROUNDS THE NET IN CELEBRATION
OF TEAMMATE UWE KRUPP'S 1996 CUP-WINNING
SHOT FOR THE COLORADO AVALANCHE AGAINST
THE FLORIDA PANTHERS IN TRIPLE OVERTIME.
AL BELLO/ALLSPORT

SHARPSHOOTER
ADAM GRAVES DEMONSTRATES A PERFECT
FOLLOW-THROUGH AS HE
UNLOADS A SLAPSHOT FROM INSIDE THE
OPPOSITION'S BLUE LINE.
BRUCE BENNETT/BRUCE BENNETT STUDIOS 1999

COMING THROUGH
WHILE DETROIT RED WING GORDIE HOWE
KEEPS MONTREAL CANADIENS
DOUG HARVEY AND CLAUDE PROVOST
OCCUPIED, TED LINDSAY SCREENS THE
MONTREAL NET, JUMPING IN ANTICIPATION
OF A TEAMMATE'S SHOT.
BRUCE BENNETT STUDIOS MID-1950S

OUTCOME INEVITABLE

NEITHER A SPRAWLING PETR SVOBODA
ON DEFENSE NOR AN OUTSTRETCHED
GARTH SNOW IN GOAL CAN KEEP THIS
SHOT FROM HEADING INTO
THE PHILADELPHIA FLYERS' NET.
SCOTT LEVY/BRUCE BENNETT STUDIOS 1997

THE AGONY

PHILADELPHIA FLYER ERIC LINDROS FEELS
THE PAIN OF LOSING TO THE
DETROIT RED WINGS IN THE FIRST GAME
OF THE STANLEY CUP FINALS.
BRUCE BENNETT STUDIOS 1997

REPARTEE

IN A SHOT THAT IS UNUSUAL FOR HAVING BEEN SNAPPED FROM THE ICE
SURFACE ONLY FEET AWAY FROM THE GOAL JUDGE'S BOX, REFEREE
RED STOREY AND DETROIT RED WING TED LINDSAY TRADE WORDS WHILE
TORONTO GOALIE HARRY LUMLEY AWAITS A VERDICT.
IMPERIAL OIL—TUROFSKY/HOCKEY HALL OF FAME MID-1950S

BIG ENTRANCE

SPARKS AND FANFARE GREET THE
PLAYERS DURING INTRODUCTIONS
BEFORE THE ALL-STAR GAME IN
SAN JOSE, CALIFORNIA.
ELSA HASCH/ALLSPORT/NHL IMAGES 1997

FOUR-GUARD SALUTE

THE ROYAL CANADIAN MOUNTED
POLICE SALUTE THE FLAGS OF CANADA
AND THE UNITED STATES BEFORE A
GAME PITTING MONTREAL
AGAINST THE BUFFALO SABRES.
CRAIG MELVIN/NHL IMAGES 1999

THE WINNINGEST KEEPER
HOISTED BY RAY BOURQUE AND ADAM
FOOTE (AND WITH SCOTT PARKER LOOKING
ON) PATRICK ROY CELEBRATES AN OVER-
TIME WIN IN WASHINGTON EARLY IN THE
SEASON. THE WIN IS THE 448TH OF ROY'S
CAREER, PUTTING HIM IN FIRST ON THE ALL-
TIME LIST, AHEAD OF TERRY SAWCHUK.
MITCHELL LAYTON/NHL IMAGES 2000

GOALIE'S CORNER
BUFFALO SABRES GOALIE DOMINIK HASEK
UNWINDS FOLLOWING THE SUPER
SKILLS COMPETITION AT THE ALL-STAR
WEEKEND IN TAMPA BAY.
CRAIG MELVIN/NHL IMAGES 1999

EYE TO EYE
Referee Bryan Lewis and Chicago
Blackhawk Bob Murray rest for a moment
as they discuss a point.
David E. Klutho/Icon Sports Media 1986

REUNITED
RETURNING TO THE GAME AFTER THREE
YEARS IN RETIREMENT, MARIO LEMIEUX
TEAMS UP WITH OLD LINEMATE JAROMIR
JAGR IN A 5-0 ROUT OF THE TORONTO
MAPLE LEAFS. COMBINED, LEMIEUX
AND JAGR PICKED UP SEVEN POINTS
ON THE NIGHT.
M. DAVID LEEDS/ALLSPORT 2000

DOM IS IN THE HOUSE
FANS GET A CLOSE-UP LOOK AT BUFFALO
SABRES GOALIE DOMINIK "THE DOMINATOR"
HASEK AS HE MAKES HIS WAY ONTO
THE ICE FROM THE DRESSING ROOM AREA
UNDER THE STANDS.
BRUCE BENNETT STUDIOS 1998

SPLIT SQUAD
PREVIOUS PAGE:
THE DETROIT RED WINGS AND THE
COLORADO AVALANCHE APPEAR TO BE
POLITELY SHARING THE SAME BENCH.
TIM DEFRISCO/NHL IMAGES 1999

PUT IT THERE, PAL
MONTREAL GOALIE GEORGE HAINSWORTH, HOLDER
OF THE SINGLE-SEASON RECORD FOR MOST
SHUTOUTS (22), POSES WITH LONG-TIME OPPONENT
ROY "SHRIMP" WORTERS OF THE NEW YORK
AMERICANS, THE FIRST GOALIE EVER TO BE NAMED
THE LEAGUE'S MOST VALUABLE PLAYER.
HOCKEY HALL OF FAME 1932

THE HERO AND THE THIEF

WHILE PHILADELPHIA FLYER TEAMMATES DON
SALESKI AND BOBBY CLARKE CHEER THE
FINAL MOMENTS OF THEIR TEAM'S STANLEY CUP
VICTORY, A FAN MAKES A MOVE TO
STEAL CLARKE'S STICK.
ASSOCIATED PRESS 1974

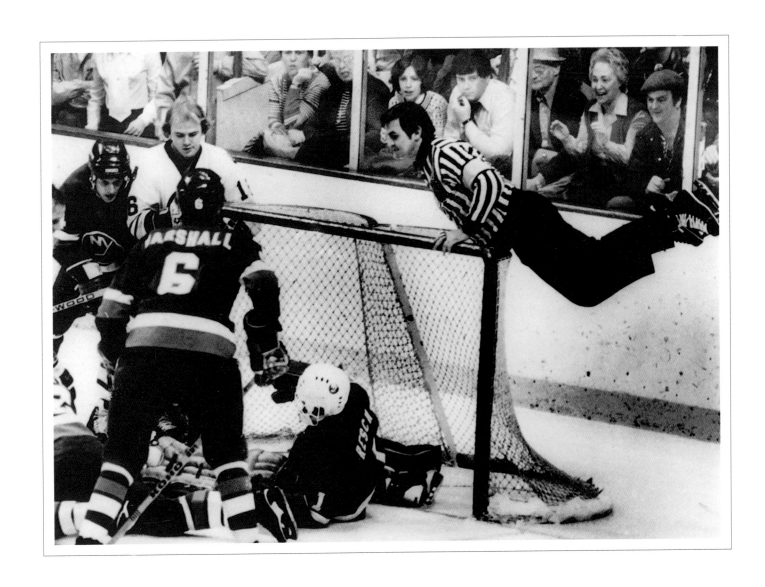

A BETTER VIEW
WITH THE PUCK BURIED IN A SCRAMBLE
IN THE CREASE OF NEW YORK
ISLANDERS GOALIE CHICO RESCH,
REFEREE JOHN McCAULEY DOES WHAT
HE CAN TO GET A CLEAR ANGLE.
UPI/NHL IMAGES 1979

THE PUCK HAS EYES

CHRIS DRURY OF THE COLORADO
AVALANCHE THREADS THE PUCK THROUGH
DALLAS STARS GOALIE ED BELFOUR FOR
THE WINNING GOAL IN GAME SIX
OF THE WESTERN CONFERENCE FINALS.
DAVID E. KLUTHO/SPORTS ILLUSTRATED 2000

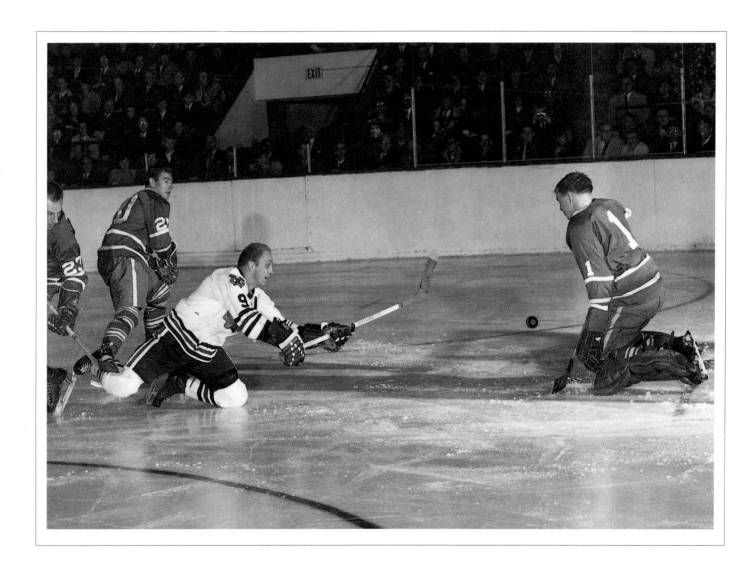

HULL DOWN

EDDIE SHACK OF THE TORONTO MAPLE LEAFS
(NO.23) PULLS THE FEET FROM UNDER CHICAGO
BLACKHAWK BOBBY HULL, WHO STILL MANAGES
TO GET A SHOT ON NET.
GRAPHIC ARTISTS/HOCKEY HALL OF FAME
EARLY TO MID-1960S

MEMORY LANE

JACQUES PLANTE'S FIRST MASK IS THE
SHOWPIECE IN THIS COLLECTION OF NHL
MEMORABILIA. IN 1950, THE PREVIOUS
YEAR'S STANLEY CUP-WINNING DETROIT
BEAT THE ALL-STARS 7-1.
DAVE SANDFORD/NHL IMAGES 1999

YOUNG PHENOM
WAYNE GRETZKY IS ALL OF 18 YEARS OLD (HALF
THE AGE OF TEAMMATE BILL FLETT, AT FAR
LEFT) AS HE WINDS DOWN HIS FIRST MAJOR LEAGUE
SEASON IN THE WORLD HOCKEY ASSOCIATION.
DAVE HUNTER, SEATED, LOOKS ON. MONTHS
LATER THE WHA MERGED WITH THE NHL.
BRUCE BENNETT/BRUCE BENNETT STUDIOS 1979

KILLER DUO

WAYNE GRETZKY AND JARI KURRI, AUTHORS OF A COM-
BINED 2,380 POINTS IN JUST EIGHT SEASONS TOGETHER
IN EDMONTON, TAKE A BREAK DURING WHAT TURNS OUT
TO BE GRETZKY'S LAST GAME WITH THE TEAM. THE PAIR
TEAMED UP ONCE MORE—FOR FIVE YEARS IN LA DURING
THE 1990S.
BRUCE BENNETT STUDIOS 1988

ALL-STAR FAN

NOTHING BUT FULL GEAR WILL DO FOR THIS
YOUNG FAN TAKING IN A PRACTICE
BEFORE THE 2001 ALL-STAR GAME
IN DENVER.
DAVE SANDFORD/NHL IMAGES 2001

DANGEROUS ANGLE
WAYNE GRETZKY, SEEN HERE IN HIS DAYS
WITH THE LOS ANGELES KINGS,
SIZES UP THE FIELD BEFORE
TAKING ON HIS FORMER TEAM, THE
EDMONTON OILERS.
ROBERT BECK/ICON SPORTS MEDIA 1992-93

APPRENTICE AND MASTER

By the time Manny Malhotra was born in 1980, Mark Messier had already played a full season in the NHL. Twenty years later, Malhotra learned to play center from his New York Ranger teammate.

Steve Babineau/Hockey Hall of Fame 2000

SHOWDOWN

Anticipation and timing are key for such top NHL faceoff men as Yanic Perreault of the Toronto Maple Leafs and Mike Modano of the Dallas Stars.

Dave Sandford/NHL Images 1999

PING

A RISING SHOT, PARTICULARLY ONE TOPPING
100 MPH, CAN CATCH EVEN THE MOST
SEASONED GOALIE OFFGUARD, INCLUDING
TORONTO NETMINDER GLENN HEALY.
DAVE SANDFORD/HOCKEY HALL OF FAME 2000

GRAVITY DELAYED

MONTREAL CANADIEN TERRY HARPER SWATS
AT A PUCK THAT SEEMS TO HOLD EVERYONE—
PLAYERS AND FANS ALIKE—IN A TRANCE.
GRAPHIC ARTISTS/HOCKEY HALL OF FAME
LATE 1960S

TENSE

IN A GAME AGAINST THE LOS ANGELES KINGS,
PETER FORSBERG AND HIS COLORADO
AVALANCHE TEAMMATES COUNT DOWN THE
SECONDS ON THE CLOCK OVERHEAD.
TIM DEFRISCO/NHL IMAGES 2000

THE KID IN CHARGE
VINCENT LECAVALIER WATCHES THE SCORE-
BOARD FROM THE TAMPA BAY LIGHTNING
BENCH. HE IS THE YOUNGEST PLAYER EVER
NAMED CAPTAIN OF A TEAM—
ONE MONTH SHY OF HIS 20TH BIRTHDAY.
DAVE SANDFORD/NHL IMAGES 2000

ROADBLOCK
NEW YORK RANGER WALT TKACZUK
(WEARING A SPECIAL HELMET TO PROTECT
AN INJURED JAW) RUNS INTO A COUPLE OF
PHILADELPHIA'S BROAD STREET BULLIES,
ANDRE DUPONT AND GARY DORNHOEFER.
LONDON LIFE—PORTNOY/HOCKEY HALL OF FAME
1973

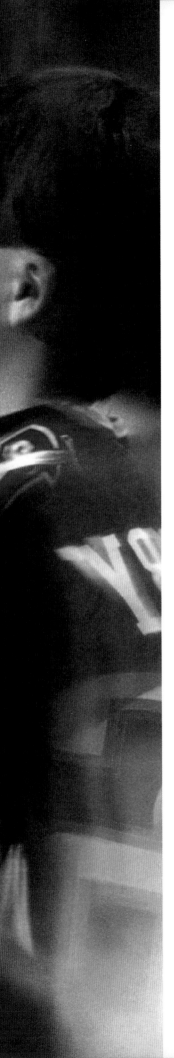

ICE DREAMS
A YOUNG BUFFALO SABRES FAN
IS JUST A SHIELD OF SAFETY
GLASS AWAY FROM HIS HOCKEY
DREAMS.
DAVE SANDFORD/NHL IMAGES 1999

PUTTIN' ON THE BRAKES
PAUL KARIYA, CAPTAIN OF THE MIGHTY
DUCKS OF ANAHEIM, MAKES A
HARD STOP AND QUICK CUTBACK ALONG
THE BOARDS.
TIM DEFRISCO/NHL IMAGES 1999

VISIBILITY ZILCH
JACQUES PLANTE, TENDING NET FOR THE
TORONTO MAPLE LEAFS LATE IN HIS
CAREER, GETS HIT WITH A SNOW SQUALL
IN FRONT OF HIS CREASE.
LONDON LIFE—PORTNOY/HOCKEY HALL OF FAME
EARLY 1970S

STAN THE MAN
CHICAGO BLACKHAWK STAN MIKITA, SHOWN HERE
IN 1973, WON FOUR SCORING TITLES
AND TWO MVP AWARDS AND AMASSED MORE
POINTS THAN ANY OTHER EUROPEAN-BORN
PLAYER IN NHL HISTORY UP TO THAT POINT.
LONDON LIFE—PORTNOY/HOCKEY HALL OF FAME 1973

CAN'T CATCH ME

JACQUES LAPERRIERE (2) AND DAVE BALON
(20) OF THE MONTREAL CANADIENS
PAIR UP IN THEIR OWN END TO CONTAIN
THE SPEEDY BOBBY HULL
OF THE CHICAGO BLACKHAWKS.
FRANK PRAZAK/HOCKEY HALL OF FAME 1966-67

IN CHECK

BOSTON BRUIN BOBBY ORR, STICK-
HANDLING WITH ONE HAND,
FENDS OFF ARNIE BROWN OF THE
NEW YORK RANGERS AS THE
TWO CUT BEHIND THE NET.
FRANK PRAZAK/HOCKEY HALL OF FAME

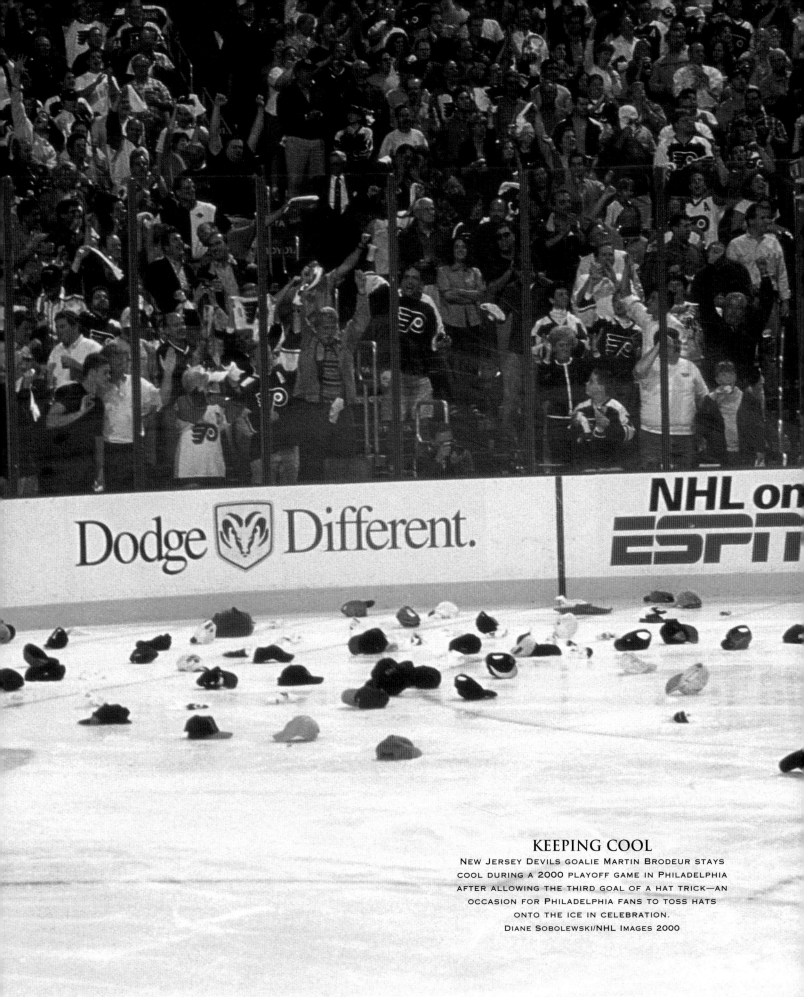

Dodge ✦ Different.

NHL on ESPN

KEEPING COOL
NEW JERSEY DEVILS GOALIE MARTIN BRODEUR STAYS
COOL DURING A 2000 PLAYOFF GAME IN PHILADELPHIA
AFTER ALLOWING THE THIRD GOAL OF A HAT TRICK—AN
OCCASION FOR PHILADELPHIA FANS TO TOSS HATS
ONTO THE ICE IN CELEBRATION.
DIANE SOBOLEWSKI/NHL IMAGES 2000

READY AND SET

NEW JERSEY DEVILS GOALIE
MARTIN BRODEUR GETS DOWN ON
ONE KNEE IN ANTICIPATION OF A
LOW SHOT FROM AN OPPONENT.
CRAIG MELVIN/NHL IMAGES 2001

SACRED GIFT

DETROIT GOALIE MIKE VERNON
STRIKES THE RITUAL POSE OF
EVERY STANLEY CUP WINNER.
RICK STEWART/ALLSPORT/NHL IMAGES
1997

BRING ON THE NEXT TEAM
AS BOB NYSTROM CHEERS FROM THE ICE
AND BUTCH GORING LEADS THE VICTORY
DANCE, NEW YORK ISLANDER JOHN TONELLI
STANDS TALL AFTER HIS OVERTIME GOAL
ELIMINATES THE PITTSBURGH PENGUINS IN
FIRST-ROUND PLAYOFF ACTION.
BRUCE BENNETT/BRUCE BENNETT STUDIOS 1982

WAYNE'S LAST ONE

ESA TIKKANEN, MARK MESSIER,
WAYNE GRETZKY, AND KEVIN LOWE
CELEBRATE THEIR FOURTH STANLEY CUP
WIN IN FIVE YEARS. DESPITE PLAYING
ANOTHER 11 SEASONS, GRETZKY
NEVER SUITED UP WITH ANOTHER
CHAMPIONSHIP TEAM.
DAVID E. KLUTHO/SPORTS ILLUSTRATED 1988

TROPHY BABY

FOUR-MONTH-OLD DAWSON MCKAY GETS TO
SHARE IN FATHER RANDY'S GLORY FOLLOWING
THE NEW JERSEY DEVILS' SIX-GAME STANLEY
CUP WIN OVER THE DALLAS STARS.
DAVID E. KLUTHO/SPORTS ILLUSTRATED 2000

DO-IT-YOURSELFER
JAROMIR JAGR OF THE PITTSBURGH
PENGUINS USES A BLOWTORCH TO SEAL
THE JOINT OF A NEW BLADE ON THE
SHAFT OF HIS STICK.
BRUCE BENNETT STUDIOS LATE 1990S

PRE-GAME WORKOUT
STRIKING AN INTERESTING POSE, AN
ATLANTA THRASHER DOES SOME LIM-
BERING UP BEFORE A GAME.
CRAIG MELVIN/NHL IMAGES 1999

QUICK AS A WINK
VANCOUVER CANUCKS GOALIE BOB
ESSENSA'S REFLEXES GET THE BETTER OF
LOS ANGELES KING LUC ROBITAILLE'S WRIST
SHOT TO THE OPEN PART OF THE NET.
JEFF VINNICK/NHL IMAGES 2001

RAH!

NEW JERSEY PLAYERS HUDDLE AND HUG
FOLLOWING A GOAL IN THE OPENING
GAME OF THE STANLEY CUP FINALS AGAINST
THE DALLAS STARS.
DIANE SOBOLEWSKI/NHL IMAGES 2000

LET IT ALL OUT

CLAUDE LEMIEUX, ONE OF ONLY FOUR
PLAYERS EVER TO WIN A STANLEY CUP
WITH THREE DIFFERENT TEAMS, ENJOYS HIS
FIRST, AS A MONTREAL CANADIEN.
BRUCE BENNETT STUDIOS 1986

MILE HIGH
THE COLORADO AVALANCHE SHARE THEIR
STANLEY CUP VICTORY WITH FANS
DURING A PUBLIC CEREMONY IN DENVER.
KEN PAPICO/ROCKY MOUNTAIN NEWS 1996

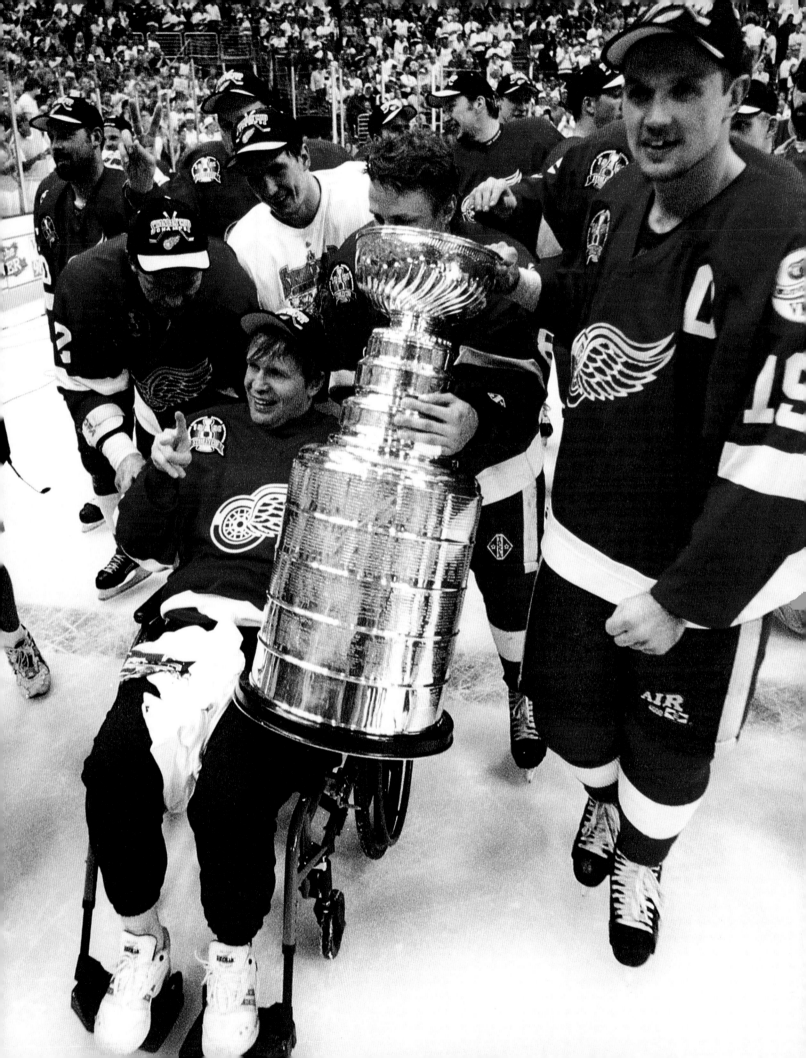

TEAMMATES FOREVER

VLADIMIR KONSTANTINOV, INJURED IN A CAR ACCIDENT
IN THE DAYS FOLLOWING HIS TEAM'S STANLEY
CUP VICTORY IN 1997, JOINS HIS DETROIT RED WING
TEAMMATES IN CELEBRATING A SECOND
CONSECUTIVE CHAMPIONSHIP ONE YEAR LATER.
ROBERT LABERGE/ALLSPORT 1998

SEASONED GREATNESS

THE 2000-2001 SEASON, PATRICK ROY'S 16TH,
ENDS UP BRINGING HIM THE BEST
SINGLE-SEASON STATISTICS OF HIS CAREER.
JEFF VINNICK/NHL IMAGES 2001

138

GUESS WHAT?
New Jersey Devil Patrick Elias, wearing teammate Petr Sykora's jersey,
calls home to the Czech Republic with
news that his team has just beaten
the Dallas Stars to win the
Stanley Cup.
Elsa Hasch/Allsport 2000

NOT A TRICK PHOTO
THREE YEARS AFTER GETTING THEIR
PROFESSIONAL START IN THEIR NATIVE SWEDEN
AT THE TENDER AGE OF 17, IDENTICAL TWINS
HENRIK AND DANIEL SEDIN HAVE BECOME CRITI-
CAL BUILDING BLOCKS FOR THE VANCOUVER
CANUCKS ORGANIZATION.
JEFF VINNICK/NHL IMAGES 2001

THE FRATERNITY
RIVALS DURING THE REGULAR SEASON, SNIPER
THEO FLEURY OF THE NEW YORK RANGERS
AND GOALIE MARTIN BRODEUR OF THE NEW
JERSEY DEVILS TEAM UP FOR NORTH
AMERICA AGAINST THE WORLD SQUAD AT
THE ALL-STAR GAME IN DENVER.
DAVE SANDFORD/NHL IMAGES 2001

JUMPING FOR JOY
New Jersey Devil Martin Brodeur is the world's
happiest goalie following teammate Jason
Arnott's Stanley Cup–winning marker in the
second overtime period of the
sixth game of the Finals against Dallas.
David E. Klutho/Sports Illustrated 2000

COUNTERFORCE
Wes Walz of the Minnesota Wild and
John Emmons of the Ottawa
Senators keep each other in check
following a face-off.
Diane Sobolewski/NHL Images 2000

TOUGH CHAMPION

Following his team's Stanley Cup
victory over the Buffalo Sabres, Mike
Modano of the Dallas Stars is captured
realizing the achievement of
a life-long dream.
Diane Sobolewski/NHL Images 1999

SAVE!

San Jose goalie Steve Shields may
be looking inside the net, but
the puck isn't there. In fact, on this
night he'll keep Vancouver
off the score sheet in a 0-0 tie.
Jeff Vinnick/NHL Images 2001

PICK A PATTERN

Decades after making its NHL debut in
Montreal, on March 10, 1955, the
Zamboni machine (named after inventor
Frank Zamboni) remains the requisite
piece of equipment to clean or
"flood" ice surfaces the world over.
Dave Sandford/NHL Images 1999

THE BOSS IS KING
HAVING PLAYED FOR TORONTO IN THE 1930S, AND
HAVING COACHED THE TEAM IN THE MID-1950S,
KING CLANCY RETURNS TO THE MAPLE LEAFS FOR
ONE MORE SEASON, AS COACH ONCE AGAIN.
GRAPHIC ARTISTS/HOCKEY HALL OF FAME 1971-72

VICTORY GREETING
DETROIT RED WINGS COACH SID ABEL (LEFT) AND
TRAINER LEFTY WILSON (RIGHT) CONGRATULATE PLAY-
ERS AS THEY RETURN TO THE TEAM DRESSING ROOM,
WITH GORDIE HOWE LEADING THE WAY AND
NORM ULLMAN BEHIND HIM.
HOCKEY HALL OF FAME/NHL IMAGES EARLY 1960S

ONE FOR THE ALBUM
WAYNE GRETZKY IS SURROUNDED BY
NEW YORK RANGER TEAMMATES ON
THE OCCASION OF HIS LAST NHL GAME.
PAUL BERESWILL/NHL IMAGES 1999

ONE LAST WAVE

WAYNE GRETZKY ACKNOWLEDGES HIS FANS
DURING POST-GAME FESTIVITIES ON THE DAY
OF HIS LAST GAME.
PAUL BERESWILL/NHL IMAGES 1999

EVERY LAST ONE A FAN

NEW YORK FANS BID THEIR FAREWELLS
TO THE GREAT ONE.
DIANE SOBOLEWSKI/NHL IMAGES 1999

LOOKING BACK

TWO YEARS BEFORE HIS RETIREMENT,
WAYNE GRETZKY CONGRATULATES TEAM-
MATE MIKE RICHTER FOR BACKSTOPPING
THE NEW YORK RANGERS TO A WIN OVER
NEW JERSEY DURING THE 1997 PLAYOFFS.

AL BELLO/ALLSPORT/NHL IMAGES 1997

HANGING 'EM UP
FOR GOOD

BACK IN THE TEAM DRESSING ROOM
FOLLOWING HIS LAST NHL GAME, WAYNE
GRETZKY SYMBOLICALLY HANGS UP
HIS SKATES.

ANDY MARLIN/BRUCE BENNETT STUDIOS 1999

THE NEXT CLASS

ON AN OUTDOOR PATCH OF ICE NORTH OF TORONTO,
JAROMIR JAGR SKATES OFF DURING THE FILMING OF THE
"POND OF DREAMS" TV SPOT FOR THE 2000 ALL-STAR
GAME. CO-STARRING WITH JAGR: PAVEL BURE, PAUL
KARIYA, ERIC LINDROS, GORDIE HOWE, WAYNE GRETZKY,
AND MARIO LEMIEUX.
TIM DEFRISCO/NHL IMAGES 2000

TITANIC TRIO

GORDIE HOWE, WAYNE GRETZKY, AND MARIO LEMIEUX
EXCHANGE HOCKEY MEMORIES DURING THE
FILMING OF THE "POND OF DREAMS" SPOT, IN WHICH
THE THREE PASS ON THE TORCH TO THE NEW STARS.
LEMIEUX HAS SINCE COME OUT OF RETIREMENT.
TIM DEFRISCO/NHL IMAGES 2000

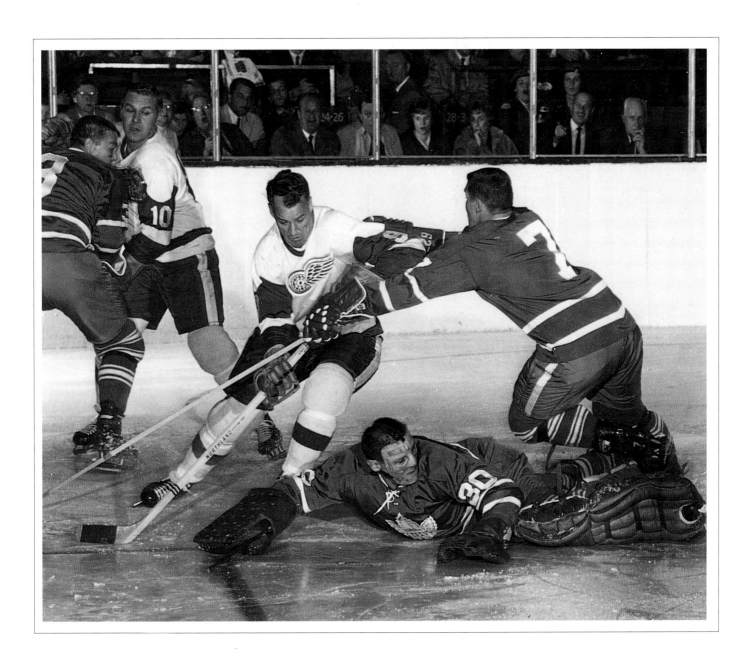

NEVER GROW OLD

A 69-YEAR-OLD GORDIE HOWE AWAITS
HIS INTRO FOR A ONE-TIME
APPEARANCE WITH THE IHL'S
DETROIT VIPERS IN A GAME AGAINST
THE KANSAS CITY BLADES. WITH
THIS GAME, MR. HOCKEY WILL HAVE
PLAYED PROFESSIONALLY IN A RECORD
SIX DIFFERENT DECADES.
TOM PIDGEON/ASSOCIATED PRESS 1997

LIVE PUCK

TORONTO GOALIE TERRY
SAWCHUK EYES THE ERRANT
PUCK AS TEAMMATE TIM
HORTON ATTEMPTS TO KEEP
GORDIE HOWE, ALSO KNOWN
AS "POWER," IN CHECK.
GRAPHIC ARTISTS/HOCKEY HALL
OF FAME 1964-65

HE'S CAUGHT THE ROCKET

GORDIE HOWE UNWINDS AFTER SCORING
THE 544TH GOAL OF HIS CAREER TO TIE
MAURICE RICHARD, A FEAT HE
ACCOMPLISHES ON HOME ICE IN DETROIT
AGAINST RICHARD'S OLD TEAM,
THE MONTREAL CANADIENS.
TONY TRIOLO/TIME INC./
SPORTS ILLUSTRATED 1963